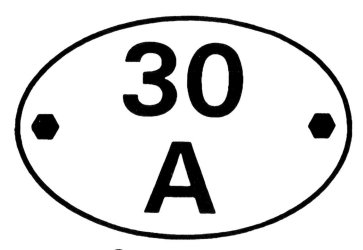

Steam on
STRATFORD SHED
in the 1950s

Just two of the Stratford locomotive stud of the 1950s, Class B12/3 4-6-0 No. 61558 and BR Standard 'Britannia' Pacific No 70034 *Thomas Hardy,* simmer outside the Jubilee Shed on 25th June 1955. Both had arrived earlier at Liverpool Street station with trains from Southend and Sheringham respectively.

Dedication

To the memory of fellow railway photographer Roy E. Wilson, in whose company the majority of the photographs contained in this book were taken.

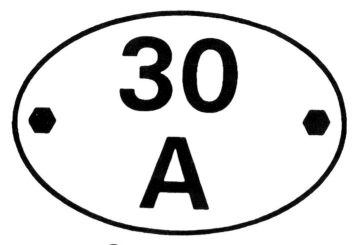

30 A

Steam on STRATFORD SHED in the 1950s

Brian Morrison

Oxford Publishing Co.

Introduction

The railway first came to Stratford in the year 1839 when the Eastern Counties Railway opened the first section of its line from Devonshire Street to Romford. It became a junction in 1840 when the Northern & Eastern Railway's grandiose plan for a trunk route from Islington to York commenced with the stretch from Bishops Stortford to Stratford. The building of the original works began shortly afterwards, utilising the ground within the fork of the Colchester and Cambridge lines known as the Polygon, and the first engine shed erected by the Northern & Eastern Railway in 1840 was known as the Polygon Shed. By 1843 a 16 road roundhouse was in evidence, together with attendant outbuildings and these survived in a number of guises well into the days of British Railways, albeit altered and extended and ultimately all but vanishing completely amid the ever-growing expansion within the Polygon of the Hudson Works buildings.

The Northern & Eastern Railway was leased to the Eastern Counties Railway from 1844 and this burgeoning network soon realised the value of the Stratford site as one ideally placed for an engineering and running shed facility close to London and astride a junction. Further building commenced in 1846 with an erecting shop that actually remained as the principal repair centre until the time of the First World War. Further land was eventually obtained for expansion with the 'New' shed being opened in 1871 and what was now the Great Eastern Railway's Jubilee Shed in 1887, the year of Queen Victoria's Golden Jubilee. This 12 road shed was exactly double the size of New Shed and was situated alongside it, separated by the usual offices, coal stages and stores buildings. The shed was enlarged in the mid-1890s following a recommendation from the Chief Mechanical Engineer, Mr J. Holden, that accommodation should be available for at least 50% of the locomotive allocation of the time (which totalled 763), and it was rebuilt completely following the end of the Second World War hostilities.

By the time that management was placed in the hands of British Railways in 1948, both the Great Eastern Railway and the LNER had contributed to a number of alterations and additions to the complex. To the north of Jubilee Shed could be found the locomotive repair shop which was often referred to as the 'New Works'. This, coupled with the number of buildings required for the old 'Hudson Works', the carriage shops, paint shop, boiler shop, engine stripping shop and transit sheds, made for an extremely large and unwieldy complex which was the largest locomotive depot in the country. Stratford was responsible for providing motive power for main line passenger workings to East Anglia, the whole of the local services from Liverpool Street and the Epping-Ongar and North Woolwich-Palace Gates branch lines. In addition there was responsibility for powering the main line freight movements, the local trips to and from Temple Mills marshalling yard as well as providing pilots for the many local depots together with Liverpool Street station itself.

The shed-code 30A was allocated to Stratford by BR in 1949 and this plate became evident on the smokebox doors of locomotives of such diversity as BR Standard 'Britannia' Pacifics and diminutive 'Y' class 0-4-0Ts. As a traditional steam shed, 30A lasted only until 1962 when dieselisation and electrification came early to eliminate steam. During the decade of the 1950s I was fortunate to be able to photograph the Stratford complex on very many occasions and was in a position to record the ever-changing scene and the many locomotive types that were always in evidence there. The site was a meandering one with, of necessity, more locomotives being housed outside the sheds than within them. The air was often choking and sulphurous and a layer of coal dust was seemingly everywhere. Not a pleasant place in which to work, but a real 'Palace of Vartieties' for the railway photographer.

Brian Morrison,
Sidcup, Kent.

A FOULIS-OPC Railway Book

© 1989 B. Morrison & Haynes Publishing Group

Reprinted 1989

Published by:
Haynes Publishing Group
Sparkford, Near Yeovil, Somerset. BA22 7JJ

Haynes Publications Inc.
861 Lawrence Drive, Newbury Park, California 91320, USA.

Printed by: J.H. Haynes & Co. Ltd.

British Library Cataloguing in Publication Data
Morrison, Brian
  30A: steam on Stratford shed in the 1950s
  1. London. Newham (London Borough).
  Stratford. Locomotive depots 1050–1060
  I. Title
  385'.314

  ISBN 0-86093-454-3

Contents

On the date that this view of 'Britannia' Pacific No. 70002 *Geoffrey Chaucer* was taken, 23rd June 1954, it was one of twelve of the class to be allocated to 30A.

Liberally coaled up for the day's work ahead as Stratford Works shunter, Class Y4 0-4-0T No. 68126 was the last of the non-Departmental types to be withdrawn in October 1957. Note the Class J20 type chimney fitted.

Bibliography

Great Eastern Railway Engine Sheds
Chris Hawkins and George Reeve (Wild Swan)

Locomotives of the L.N.E.R.
Railway Correspondence & Travel Society (RCTS)

Railways of the Eastern Region
Geoffrey Body (Patrick Stephens)

BR Steam Motive Power Depots
Paul Bolger (Ian Allan)

LNER Sheds in Camera
John Hooper (Oxford Publishing Co.)

The Riddles Standard Types in Traffic
G. Freeman Allen (George Allen & Unwin)

Locomotives at the Grouping
H.C. Casserley & S.W. Johnston (Ian Allan)

B.R. Steam Locomotives from Nationalisation to Modernisation
Alan Williams and David Percival (Ian Allan)

Riddles and the 9Fs
Colonel H.C.B. Rogers (Ian Allan)

BR Standard Steam in Close-Up
Tony Fairclough & Alan Wills (D. Bradford Barton)

London Midland Steam Locomotives, Volumes 1 & 2
Brian Morrison (D. Bradford Barton)

London Steam in the Fifties
Brian Morrison (Ian Allan)

ABC British Railways Locomotives – Various Editions (Ian Allan)

Trains Illustrated Magazines – Various Issues (Ian Allan)

Awaiting Works Attention

The background building shown here still stands today as Stratford Major Depot, undertaking heavy repairs to present day BR traction. In the 1950s however, it was known as the 'New Works' or, more formerly, the Stratford Locomotive and Carriage Works. Either way the building always had a line of locomotives outside awaiting attention of one sort or another and on 31st August 1957, Class D16/3 4-4-0 No. 62576 heads a line-up which also includes a 'Sandringham' Class 4-6-0, a WD 2-8-0 and a J17 0-6-0.

(Above) Looking like a precursor to Gresley's *Flying Scotsman* of the 1960s with two tenders, Class B2 4-6-0 No. 61617 *Ford Castle* awaits entry to the Works on 25th June 1955. The second tender, was actually owned by another member of the class which was being worked upon inside the building.

(Opposite top) On 29th November 1954 a Class F4 2-4-2T No. 67174, a T.W. Worsdell Great Eastern design dating from 1884, which had been sent down from its allocated shed of Yarmouth (South Town), awaits entry to the Works for a decision to be made as to its continued service. In fact the old stager never emerged, being cut up soon afterwartds.

(Right) Rebuilt from a Belpair boilered Class D16/2 4-4-0 to a D16/3 with a larger round-topped boiler, No. 62601 still retains its original decorative valancing on 31st August 1956, awaiting entry to the Works. The locomotive was built at Stratford in February 1911 and cut up there following withdrawal in January 1957.

(Opposite top) A vintage J. Holden Great Eastern design and a Gresley LNER type stand side by side outside the large Works building on 29th January 1955. The little Class J66 0-6-0T originally carried number 68382 before being taken into Departmental Stock upon withdrawal in 1952 and re-numbered 31. The Class J39/1 0-6-0, No. 64767 was allocated to 30A at this time.

(Left) The Winter 1955/6 edition of Ian Allan's *ABC of British Railways Locomotives* lists 85 Class N7 0-6-2Ts as being allocated to 30A, with more of the class being attached to the other Stratford District sheds of Hertford East, Bishops Stortford, Southend Victoria and Colchester. On this basis it is obvious that many of the fleet total of 135 could be seen there at any one time, as with N7/3 No. 69676 requiring attention in a line of locomotives awaiting entry to the Works on 22nd August 1954.

(Right) Allocated to Ipswich shed (32B), this photograph of Class J67/2 0-6-0T No. 68572 rather gives the impression that a decision had already been made to scrap it as the roof of the cab had been removed, probably to fit to another engine of Class J67 or J69. However, the locomotive was not officially withdrawn from stock until November 1954, over two months after this view which dates from September of that year.

Awaiting admission to the Works in January 1955 is a J. Holden Class E4 2-4-0 No. 62795. Allocated to Cambridge (31A) at the time, it was destined not to return there as a decision to scrap the engine must have been made shortly after this photograph was taken, the official withdrawal date being given as March of that year.

Under Repair

Inside Stratford Works on 7th July 1956, a Thompson Class L1 2-6-4T No. 67740 from Neasden shed (34E) is the subject of overhaul, together with Class B1 4-6-0 No. 61052.

With most of the locomotive inside the Works receiving attention, what remains of Class J69/1 0-6-0 No. 68556 makes an unusual sight in the Works yard. This view looks as if it would be more suitable for the *On the Scrap Line* section which follows but, in reality, this engine was not to be withdrawn from service until another nine years had elapsed from the date when this photograph was taken, 5th September 1953.

The smokebox door from Norwich (32A) based Class B1 4-6-0 No. 61312 waits to be reunited with its owner which is undergoing major repair on 7th July 1956.

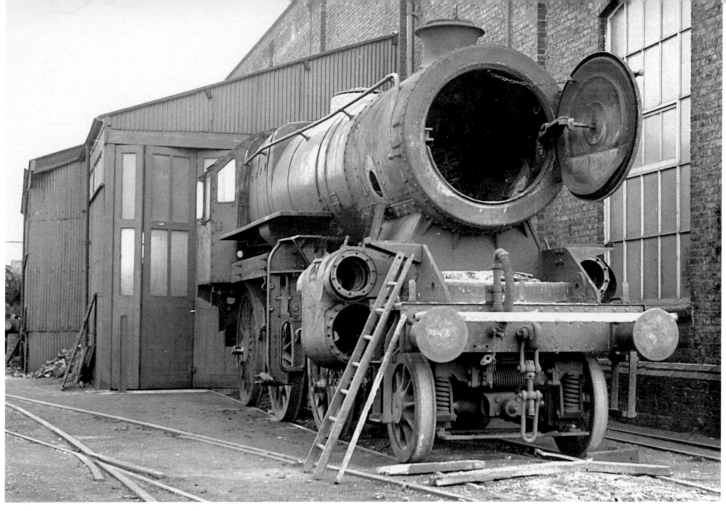

Works capacity was invariably at a premium in the 1950s and if parts of a locomotive could be removed outside the premises and worked upon on the inside without the engine itself needing to be taken under cover, this was a means to relieve pressure of space, particularly during the summer months. On 22nd August 1954 an Ivatt Class 4MT 2-6-0 receives attention with all the valve gear and connecting rods removed and the boiler tubes partly withdrawn.

On 29th May 1954, Cambridge (31A) allocated Class D16/3 4-4-0 No. 62545 is in course of repair outside the Works building. This was just one of many engines that were born and died at Stratford, this example having been constructed there in January 1904 and finishing up on the scrap line over 54 years later, in September 1958.

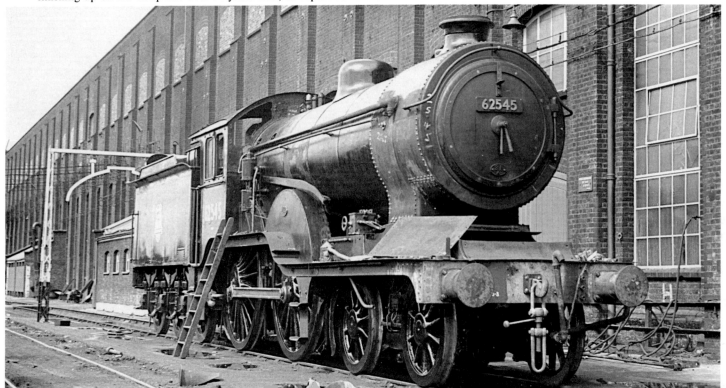

On the Scrap Line

The name *Claud Hamilton* was originally given to Class D14 4-4-0 No. 1900 in March 1900, Lord Claud Hamilton then being the Chairman of the Great Eastern Railway for whom he served on the Board for over 50 years. When it was decided in 1933 to rebuild the locomotive with a Gresley boiler and piston valves, the name was perpetuated but the original London & North Western Railway style plates were changed to the LNER pattern. The engine was rebuilt to a D15 and then to a D16/3 and withdrawn in 1947 with the nameplates being transferred to No. 62546 which survived in service until June 1957. With the nameplates and builder's plates removed, the locomotive awaits its fate on the scrap line outside Stratford Works on 13th September 1957.

In the 1950s steam locomotives were scrapped in the everyday course of things with their numbers sometimes building up for weeks or even months until time could be found to remove any useful parts from them, and then cut up what remained for scrap purposes. The Class J70 0-6-0T tram engines were designed for use along public roads on the Wisbech & Upwell Tramway and latterly on the line from Yarmouth Vauxhall station that ran along a main road to the fish wharf. Constructed for the Great Eastern Railway at Stratford from 1903, eleven of the twelve vehicles which made up the class survived to receive a British Railways number and the last was withdrawn from its then Colchester (30E) allocation in August 1955. No. 68219 was taken out of service in August 1953 and is seen here awaiting scrapping at Stratford on 5th September of that year.

Flanked by Class F6 2-4-2T No. 67221 and Class E4 2-4-0T No. 62783, Class C12 4-4-2T No. 67360 is stored with the mandatory covering over the chimney and awaits its fate on the scrap line. The Class C12s were an Ivatt design for the Great Northern Railway, dating from 1899, and this example was finally withdrawn in January 1955 after working with other Cambridge-based members of the class on Great Eastern metals where they handled the Saffron Walden trains, the Cambridge-Sudbury-Colchester cross-country services and the Swaffam-Thetford and Bury St Edmunds-Long Melford branch lines.

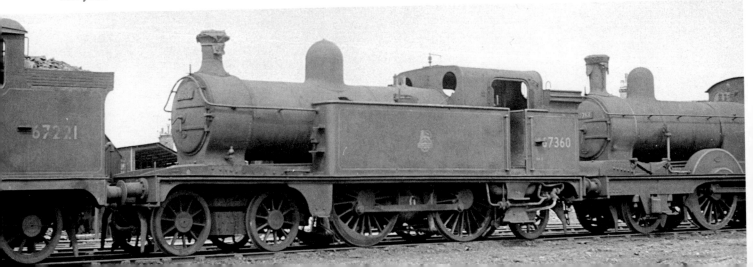

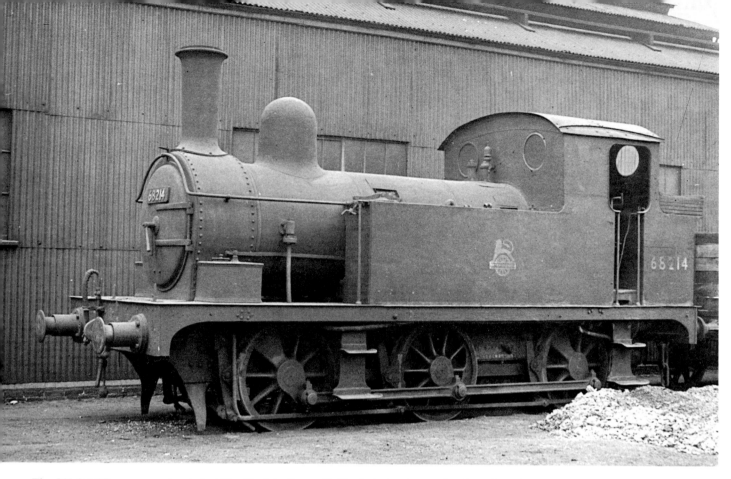

The J65 0-6-0Ts were constructed at Stratford to James Holden's design in two batches of ten in 1889 and 1893 and originally classified as E22. They became known as 'Blackwall Tanks' in view of their association with the Fenchurch Street-Blackwall line where a 15 minute interval service once operated daily from early morning until 7pm! Only four of the class survived to be allocated a BR number following Nationalisation in 1948 and all but one of these were withdrawn from service between 1948 and 1953. No. 68214 avoided the cutting torch until October 1956, being retained at Yarmouth Beach shed (32F) as spare engine for the quay lines. The locomotive is shown here on the Stratford scrap line on 17th November 1956.

The first of the LNER classified J16/J17 0-6-0s was built by the Great Eastern at Stratford in 1900, and the complete fleet of 90 locomotives was originally allocated to either March or Peterborough sheds for working the heavy freight and coal trains of the day. Having been rebuilt with Belpaire boilers, all the J16s were re-classified to J17 by 1932 and the fleet continued to be the mainstay of these services until well after the Grouping of 1923, the last one not being withdrawn by British Railways until September 1963. The first example of the class to be officially withdrawn from BR ownership in September 1954 was No. 65547 although, in fact, the locomotive concerned was already awaiting scrapping at Stratford without its tender on 22nd August of that year.

(Top) A Robinson design for the Great Central Railway, the Class L3 2-6-4Ts were the first locomotives with this substantially popular wheel arrangement to be introduced into this country, being constructed at Gorton Works during the early years of World War 1 and intended for heavy freight and mineral haulage. No. 69060 was withdrawn from Frodingham shed (36C) in June 1954 and was a surprise visitor to Stratford on 22nd August 1954 where it had arrived to be put into use as a stationary boiler for the Carriage Works there. (Above) Having acted in this capacity for a further three years, the engine was finally cut up at Stratford Works. Another photograph on the scrap line was possible on 31st August 1957, however, before this took place.

(Above) Withdrawn in September 1954, Class E4 2-4-0 No. 62783 awaits final oblivion on the scrap line on 29th January 1955. Just 18 members of the original class of 100 locomotives survived to receive a BR number in 1948 and all these remained in service until 1954 when LMS 2MT 2-6-0s and diesel railcars were introduced which were able to operate within the high 'Route Availability 2' categories applying to a number of lines in East Anglia.

(Below) The last of the two rather strange Class Y11 0-4-0 petrol engines constructed by the Motor Rail and Tram Car Company, No. 15099, awaits the final curtain outside Stratford Works on 17th November 1956. The machines were chain driven with a two-speed gearbox and were built between 1922 and 1925. Taken into the stock of the North British Railway and the LNER respectively, they remained unclassified until 1943.

Freshly painted in un-lined black livery, three locomotives are towed away from the Stratford Works paintshop on a sunny 29th January 1955 by Class J68 0-6-0T No. 68639. The leading engine is a Class J39/1 0-6-0 No. 64766 which is coupled to Class J69/1 0-6-0T No. 68491 with Class N2/2 0-6-2T No. 69533 bringing up the rear. At this time the locomotives were allocated to Stratford, Cambridge and Hornsey sheds respectively.

Two Class J17 0-6-0s and two Class K5 Moguls are pictured outside the Works on 25th June 1955 and it is obvious which two have been overhauled there and which two await entry! The J17s are No. 65576 and, with a smaller tender, No. 65514. The Moguls are Nos 61817 and 61815, both allocated to Stratford.

The fresh paintwork given to Hill Class J20/1 0-6-0 No. 64689 fairly glistens under a hot sun on 11th August 1954. All 25 of the class spent most of their working life allocated to Stratford, Cambridge and March sheds although, surprisingly, some visited both Darlington and Doncaster Works for attention between 1926 and 1930.

Fitted with steam brake and vacuum operated push-pull gear in 1949 for working the Epping-Ongar services, Class F5 2-4-2T No. 67193 waits for the fire to be relit following Works overhaul on 25th June 1955. The ugly stove pipe chimney that is fitted is slightly compensated for by the fresh black paintwork being attractively lined out.

Originally constructed at Stratford in 1912 as the first of ten Class J18 0-6-0s, No. 64640 was one of four that were re-built to a Class J19/1 with a Belpaire boiler, and then re-built again to its final form of Class J19/2 with a Diagram 28A boiler with round-topped firebox. In this form the class was eventually to total 35 locomotives. Having been completely overhauled and re-painted at Stratford on 23rd January 1954, the engine, the first goods type on the GER ever to carry a superheated boiler, awaits coal and water before making a way back to its home shed of March (31B).

(Top) Although Stratford was the works responsible for the creation of the Class N7 design, oddly enough they did not actually construct any of them after appearance of the original types, the LNER using Doncaster and Gorton Works and some outside contractors to build the final 112 of the 134 engines. Built at Doncaster in December 1927, Class N7/3 No. 69711 has its bunker refilled with coal from the massive Stratford coaler after overhaul at Stratford on 11th August 1954. The coaler was taken down, piece by piece, in 1963.

(Above) At the time of the amalgamation in 1923 all the Great Eastern Railway Class J67/J69 0-6-0Ts were naturally allocated to GER sheds, the likes of Stratford, Cambridge, Colchester, Ipswich, Norwich, Lowestoft, Yarmouth and King's Lynn. By Nationalisation in 1948, however, their allocations had diversified to a quite remarkable extent with examples being found in far flung LNER outposts such as Perth, Glasgow Eastfield, Wrexham, Liverpool, Trafford Park, Doncaster, Immingham and Lincoln. It was from Lincoln (40A) that Class J69/1 No. 68541 was sent to Stratford for overhaul and had just emerged from the shops when photographed there on 25th June 1955.

Having received a full overhaul and repaint at Stratford, Class B12/3 4-6-0 No. 61580 has been coaled up and awaits firing prior to returning to its home shed of Grantham (35B) on 22nd August 1954. As GER Class S69 No. 8580, this locomotive was the last of the class to be constructed and entered service in October 1928, 17 years after the first of the type appeared from Stratford in 1911. This particular locomotive, however, was built by Beyer Peacock & Co.

(Below) Resplendent in freshly applied black paint and new-style BR emblem, Class J15 0-6-0 No. 65453 was coaled up and fired when recorded at Stratford on 31st August 1957 after emerging from the Works. Visually the engine belied that it was a veteran performer of over half a century of use.

(Above) Possibly it was imagination, but Stratford Works seemed to take just a little more trouble with the paint finish of locomotives that carried a 30A shed plate. Maybe the rubbing down of the metalwork prior to painting was undertaken more energetically or perhaps there was some truth in the rumour that they always carried two types of black paint, the more lasting and expensive one being for those with a Stratford allocation! With that special finish, Class J17 0-6-0 No. 65508 was outside New Shed on 11th August 1954, one of 16 of the class fitted with a small tender.

(Opposite top) Constructed at Darlington Works in October 1924, Class K3/2 Mogul No. 61817 was allocated to Stratford when photographed there following overhaul on 25th June 1955.

(Opposite middle) Fitted with a tender cab, or back cab, to give the footplate crew some protection from the elements when working tender first on the Thetford-Swaffam branch, the new black paint applied in Stratford Works to Class E4 2-4-0 No. 62788 glints in the evening sunshine of 5th September 1953.

(Opposite bottom) Awaiting return to its home shed of Lowestoft (32C) following works overhaul, Class F5 2-4-2T No. 67216 awaits coaling up on 29th May 1954 in company with immaculate Class N7/1 0-6-2T No. 69646. The F5 Class remained intact until the following year when withdrawal proceeded quite rapidly, the type becoming extinct by May 1958.

All the 'Claud Hamilton' Class 4-4-0s were built at Stratford between 1900 and 1923, with this example being one of the last to emerge in August 1923. Retaining decorative valancing to the end, No. 62618 had just emerged from works overhaul there when recorded in June 1955. With the engine being withdrawn in November 1959, this overhaul probably transpired to be the final one.

A King's Cross (34A) allocated N2/2 0-6-2T No. 69493 stands in Jubilee Shed yard on 10th March 1956 alongside Class B1 4-6-0 No. 61226. Members of Class N2 from the Great Northern Section generally visited Doncaster Works for repair and overhaul but some were attended to at Stratford, a practise that commenced in 1936 and did not cease until May 1958.

'Thundersley'

The last remaining original London, Tilbury & Southend Railway 79 class 4-4-2T was No. 80 of the batch constructed in 1909. Until the amalgamation of 1923 the class consisted of 16 engines, all of which carried names associated with towns served by the LT&S such as *Stratford, Forest Gate, Leytonstone, Shoeburyness, Westcliff* and *Thundersley*. To commemorate the centenary of the opening of the line to Southend, London Midland Region Class 3P No. 41966 was rescued from Toton (18A) and sent to Derby Works where the locomotive was beautifully recreated to almost the original condition in which it first appeared from Robert Stephenson's works. At that time the engine was the winner of a gold medal at the 1909 Imperial International Exhibition held at London's White City, albeit temporarily named *Southend-on-Sea*. Prior to a special commemorative run from Southend to Liverpool Street on 3rd March 1956, which was repeated the following week when the weather was much improved, *Thundersley* was maintained at Stratford and photographed there on both 10th and 11th March 1956 replete in Tilbury bright green with red-brown underframes. The engine is now preserved by the National Railway Museum and loaned to Bressingham Steam Museum.

The 'Standards' Arrive

(Above) Early in 1951 the first of the new British Railways Standard classes appeared from Crewe Works, a two-cylinder Class 7 Mixed Traffic Pacific No. 70000 *Britannia*. After the naming ceremony at Marylebone station on 31st January, the locomotive went straight to Stratford for operation of the Liverpool Street-Norwich services. Now preserved, this portrait of the engine was taken at Stratford on 10th March 1956.

(Left) 'Britannia' Class 7MT Pacific No. 70003 *John Bunyan* was another of the Stratford allocation of twelve such locomotives for the Norwich services. It was awaiting its next duty outside Jubilee Shed on 22nd August 1954 when photographed alongside the first of Thompson's Class B1 4-6-0s, No. 61000 *Springbok*.

Constructed at Doncaster and Horwich Works from 1953, just five of the 115 BR Standard Class 4MT Moguls were allocated to Stratford when this photograph was taken on 23rd January 1954 of No. 76030 peering from the murk of New Shed. A standardised version of Ivatt's Class 4MT Mogul for the LMS and London Midland Region, they were considered as better looking than their predecessors due to the drop plate shown descending from the running plate to the buffer beam, which eliminated the stark angular-looking front end of the Ivatt machines.

Another of the 30A allocation of Britannia Pacifics, No. 70037 *Hereward the Wake*, receives minor attention inside Jubilee Shed on 7th July 1956.

Considered by many to be one of Riddles most successful designs, the BR Standard 9F 2-10-0s eventually totalled 251 locomotives with construction undertaken by Crewe and Swindon from 1954 to 1958. The type was never particularly prolific on Great Eastern metals and, when this view of No. 92014 was taken at Stratford on 23rd June 1954, it was the only locomotive of the fleet allocated to 30A.

Class 4MT Mogul No. 76030 is seen outside Jubilee Shed on 23rd April 1955. In company with all the BR standard designs, these engines were much easier to service than the older types; self-cleaning smokeboxes, drop grates and hopper ash pans all helping to ease the fireman's chores at the end of a shift. For the drivers there was less preparation needed with such equipment fitted as mechanical lubricators and grease nipples on the mechanical parts.

With an excellent pedigree emanating from the highly successful Fowler tanks through their Stanier and Fairburn developments, another first class Riddles' standard design was the 4MT 2-6-4Ts of which 155 were constructed at Brighton, Derby and Doncaster between 1951 and 1956. Receiving an Intermediate Overhaul inside Stratford Works on 7th July 1956, No. 80070 was then one of the Tilbury (33B) allocation.

Departmental Stock

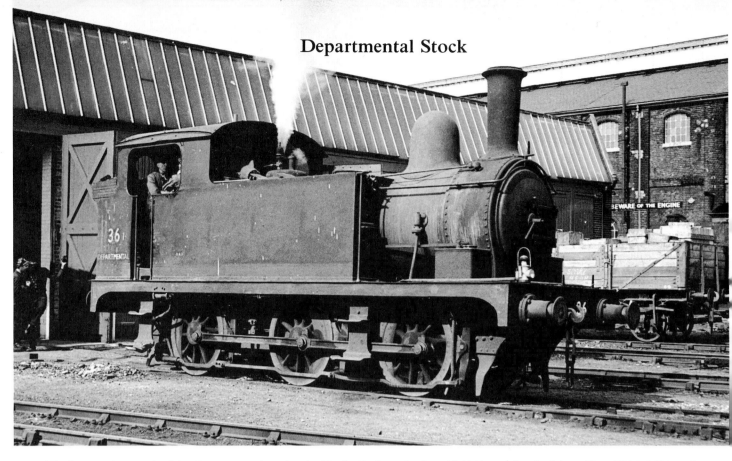

The locomotives retained for Departmental use by the Works Engineer in the mid-1950s consisted of three Class J66 0-6-0Ts and one Class Y4 0-4-0T. Carrying Departmental number 36, this Class J66 engine was withdrawn from the running stock in September 1952 as No. 68378 and finally scrapped in January 1959.

Known locally as the 'Stratford Pot', this Class Y4 0-4-0T No. 33 in Departmental stock once carried the number 68129 even though it spent its entire existence from 1921, when new as a service locomotive for Stratford Works, being numbered in Great Eastern stock as 7210.

(Above) Watering up from the 'Heath Robinson' type contraption used for the purpose by Departmental stock outside their own small shed on 23rd June 1954, is another of the Class J66 tanks, No. 32. Having carried number 7281 in GER days and 8370 (and later 68370 from Nationalisation), this particular engine was already in service stock at the 1923 Grouping and was not finally withdrawn until September 1962.

(Below) The two-road shed maintained at Stratford for the use of engines employed in the Works came under the direction of the Works Engineer and was entirely separate from the Running Department. Constructed prior to the First World War, it could house four tanks under cover and was not finally demolished until the 1980s. Crews for the Departmental engines were usually former Running Department men who, after transfer, remained separate to such an extent that a Running Department 'pilot' was required when one of the service locomotives had to cross the main line between the old and new parts of the Works, with the Works Engineer being duly invoiced for the service! On 29th January 1955, Class J66 0-6-0Ts Nos 31 and 32 await use alongside push-and-pull fitted Class F5 2-4-2T No. 67218.

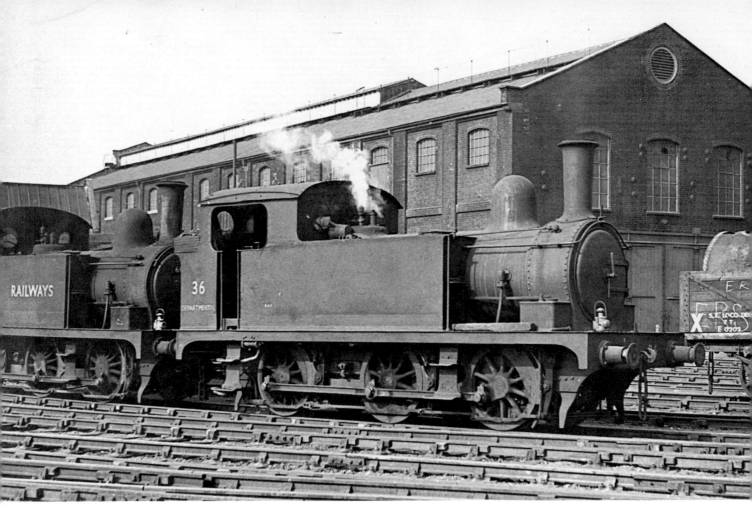

(Above) Introduced to the Great Eastern Railway as Class T18 in 1886, what was to become the Class J66 0-6-0Ts once totalled 50 in number, all being built at Stratford in two years up to 1888. Nineteen survived to receive a LNER number and all these in turn came into British Rail stock in 1948. No. 68378 was numbered into service stock in 1952 as Departmental No. 36 and was photographed shunting the Works yard on 10th April 1954.

(Above) Seemingly superfluous to the works duties of the day, Departmental Class J66 0-6-0T No. 32 looks out of the diminutive Works Shed on a January day in 1955, still sporting a smokebox number plate in addition to the number being painted on the buffer beam.

(Opposite) When transferred to works service stock in 1952, the three Class J66 tanks took over the duties of the Holden Class J92 0-6-0 crane tanks, which were themselves a rebuild of the original Ruston & Proctor 0-6-0Ts, originally introduced as long ago as 1868 and which held sway there, identified as B, C and D until withdrawal. Originally numbered 68382, Departmental No. 31, once employed as a Boston Docks shunter, is seen in profile on 10th April 1954.

Nameplates

With royal permission given, the first of the new 4-6-0s built by the LNER from 1928 to work express passenger services in the Eastern counties was named *Sandringham* and the whole class subsequently became known as 'Sandringhams'. At Stratford on 23rd June 1954, the locomotive carrying the plate was now classified B17/6 and numberd 61600.

In 1948 the newly nationalised British Railways agreed to take over from the Ministry of Supply the 733 'Austerity' 2-8-0 freight engines then in Great Britain which had been designed by Robert A. Riddles during the 1939-45 war, when he had had the position of Deputy Director of Royal Engineer Equipment. The locomotives were originally intended for war service overseas. The last of these functional and free steaming engines to be built was numbered 90732 and was the only one of the massive fleet to carry a name, *Vulcan*, in recognition of the fact that the majority were built at Vulcan Foundry, Newton-le-Willows. The plate, which was high up on the cabside, was photographed on the locomotive at Stratford on 5th September 1953.

The first of Thompson's Class B1 4-6-0s was constructed in 1942 and given the name *Springbok* as its completion coincided with a visit to these shores by General Smuts, the Prime Minister of South Africa. Succeeding locomotives of the type were also given names of various species of antelope and, initially, they were known as the 'Antelope' class. However, the policy had to be abandoned as there was nothing like 400 plus types of antelope known to mankind, but there were over 400 of the class constructed! In the end 40 engines were given such names, ranging from the pleasant *Gazelle, Impala, Eland* and *Roedeer* to distinctly strange titles such as *Bongo, Puku, Nilghai, Chiru* and *Dibatag*. This plate of No. 61000 was recorded at Stratford on 23rd June 1954.

In the late Eric Treacy's classic Ian Allan publication *Steam Up* of 1948, he asked if a class of express locomotives could be named to reflect British heritage and be known as 'Britannia'. His wish came about in 1951 when, to coincide with the Festival of Britain, the first of the new BR Standard 7MT Pacifics appeared as No. 70000 *Britannia*. The fifth member of the class was No. 70004 *William Shakespeare*.

All the 'Sandringham' 4-6-0s were named but not all received plates appertaining to large country houses belonging to members of the peerage, some being named after regiments and others after Association Football clubs. *Holkham* was attached to No. 61601, *Leicester City* to No. 61665 and *The Essex Regiment* to No. 61658.

K5 – Only Child

In 1943 details appeared for rebuilding the three-cylinder Gresley Class K3 Mogul fleet with two Class B1 type cylinders. The total cylinder volume being less, it was necessary to increase boiler pressure in order to maintain the tractive effort and new boilers were ordered. Class K3 No. 206 was selected for the rebuilding and very little of the original engine was retained as, apart from the boiler and cylinder, the frames, driving wheels and buffers were all new, the rebuilt engine just retaining its original cab and chimney, albeit with a shorter blast pipe. Following trials lasting some two years, it was reported that the locomotive, which had been designated Class K5, had superior riding to the K3s and that shed maintenance was easier due to the accessibility of the two outside cylinders and motion. Whilst the rebuild was a success, therefore, these advantages over the Class K3 did not warrant the considerable length of time taken for the work to be done and further rebuilding was suspended, the K5 remaining as a solitary example of its type until withdrawn in 1960. Originally allocated to New England shed, Peterborough (35A), it received BR number 61863 and was transferred to Stratford in 1954 where these views were taken on 29th May 1954 and 23rd April 1955 respectively.

Ex-Great Eastern Types

Considering their 0-4-0T wheel arrangement, the five A.J. Hill Dock Tanks were quite large and powerful engines. Built at Stratford in 1913 by the Great Eastern Railway, they worked in the East London area throughout their lives and were finally withdrawn between 1955 and 1957 but with the Departmental Stock locomotive No. 33, surviving until closure of the Old Works in 1963. On 10th March 1956, No. 68128 commences to haul trucks away from one of the Stratford coal lines after loading by crane. A far cry from the methods of loading and unloading offered by today's modern 'merry-go-round' facilities.

Recorded at Stratford just prior to being transferred to Hitchin (34D) in November 1954, Class E4 2-4-0 No. 62785 then had a spell of duty hauling Henlow Camp trains on the Midland Railway tracks of the Bedford branch. This engine was the very last of the class to be withdrawn from service in December 1959, when it was beautifully restored to original Great Eastern condition at Stratford. Carrying its original number of 490, it was sent to the Transport Museum at Clapham and now rests in the National Railway Museum at York.

Thirty Class J68 0-6-0Ts were constructed, twenty for the Great Eastern Railway between 1912 and 1914 and a further ten LNER engines after the Grouping of 1923. No. 68662 blows off steam at Stratford on 10th April 1954 while taking a respite from shunting duties.

0-6-0 Tender Engines

The Great Eastern Railway fleet of Class Y14 0-6-0s was built from 1883 to 1913 to the design of T. W. Worsdell and eventually totalled 289 engines, numerically the largest class on the GER system. Of these 272 survived to become LNER Class J15 at the Grouping of 1923 and a remarkable 127 were handed over to British Railways in 1948, the final one not being withdrawn until 1962. On 31st August 1957, No. 65476 rolls into Stratford shed having arrived earlier at Temple Mills Yard with a short freight from East Anglia. Class B1 4-6-0 No. 61399 can be seen in the background.

Of the 90 engines constructed at Stratford that became LNER Class J17, all but one entered BR stock in 1948, No. 8200 having been extensively damaged by a German V2 rocket at Stratford in November 1944 and subsequently withdrawn. On 1st August 1954, No. 65531 basks in the evening sunshine having arrived earlier with a freight from its home depot of Colchester (30E).

All 35 of the Class J19 0-6-0s designed by Holden for the GER passed into BR ownership and received their new numbers in the 60000 series. Colchester-allocated No. 64666 stands at the east end of Jubilee Shed on 29th January 1955, exactly six years prior to official withdrawal.

In 1941, replacement boilers were required for the 25 Hill locomotives that made up the Class J20 0-6-0s, plus the remaining unrebuilt Class B12s that were exiled on the Great North of Scotland lines. A LNER standard type boiler was constructed with a round-topped firebox instead of a Belpaire, and the first example was fitted in 1943 to No. 8292 (BR No. 64697) with the last in January 1956 to this engine, No. 64676, photographed at Stratford on 29th May 1954 still retaining the Belpaire variety. The delay of some 13 years before this locomotive was modified came to an end when the Scottish based Class B12s were eventually withdrawn and the remaining boilers were at last dispatched to Stratford!

N7 Variants

Twelve locomotives made up Hill's GER Class L77 0-6-2Ts at the 1923 Grouping, all being built at Stratford. Becoming LNER Class N7, a further 122 were constructed between 1923 and 1928 utilising the facilities of Gorton and Doncaster Works in addition to private contractors R. Stephenson and W. Beardmore. The classification N7/1 was given to the post-Grouping engines of the original design, of which No. 69627 was an example at Stratford on 7th July 1956.

The Classification N7/2 was given to the locomotives constructed in 1926-27 with redesigned motion to increase valve travel from 3³/₈in to a fraction under 5³/₄in and one of the engines in this category was No. 69689 which was constructed by William Beardmore & Co. of Dalmuir in 1927. This engine was the very first of the N7 fleet to be withdrawn from service in March 1957 and when this photograph was taken a short time later, the rear portion of the right side connecting rod had already been removed for fitting to another of the class. Observe the two sunken footsteps built into the high-sided bunker and the absence of coal rails.

Classification N7/3 denoted the locomotives which were constructed at Doncaster in 1927-1928 with a change in boiler design to include a round-topped firebox in accordance with contemporary LNER standards. The category also included Class N7/2 locomotives which were rebuilt in this fashion from 1943. On 11th August 1954, fresh from Stratford Works, No. 69725 retains the oval Doncaster Works plate on the front splasher. When steam workings ceased south of March in September 1962, this locomotive was one of the eight survivors of the class to be finally withdrawn.

The locomotives that made up classification N7/4 were the original Stratford built Great Eastern ones which were rebuilt between 1940 and 1949 with new round-topped boilers but retained their original short travel valves. One of this type was No. 69614 seen at Stratford on 29th May 1954 showing the large Westinghouse pump on the right side of the smokebox.

The final category, N7/5, came about from 1943 when the Class N7/1s were given new boilers with a round-topped firebox but retained short valve travel. Just out-shopped from Stratford Works in lined-out black livery on the same day, one of these types, Gorton built No. 69646, was another of the eight class survivors that were not finally withdrawn until September 1962.

The 2-4-2Ts

The locomotives that became LNER Class F4 were the survivors of an original T.W. Worsdell design of 1884 modified by J. Holden, plus those built under S.D. Holden to the same design between 1903 and 1909. Withdrawal of the Worsdell engines commenced as early as the year 1913 with the last going in 1929. During this year the first of the later J. Holden engines was withdrawn from service but it was not until 1956 that the class became extinct. On 5th September 1953, Class F4 2-4-2T No. 67176 stands outside Stratford Works awaiting the cutter's torch, having been withdrawn three months earlier.

Class F5 was made up of 30 engines rebuilt from Holden's Class F4 series between 1911 and 1920 with boilers having an increased pressure. Withdrawn in November 1955, No. 67217 had just over one year left in service when photographed at Stratford in October 1954.

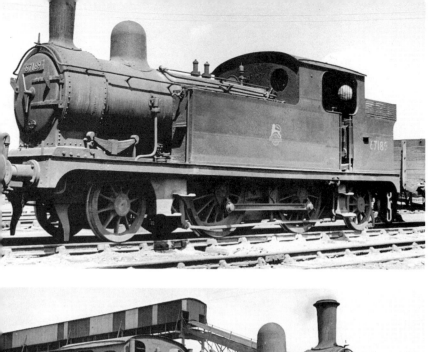

One of the Class F5s allocated to Colchester (30E), No. 67189 awaits works attention on 7th July 1956 but, in fact, never received it as withdrawal came about in December of that year. Note the short stove-pipe chimney fitted to the locomotive which does absolutely nothing for its aesthetics.

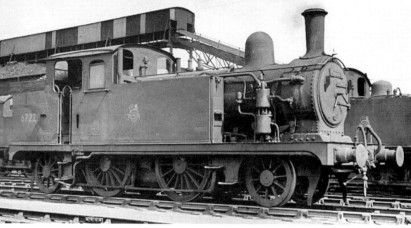

(Left) S.D. Holden's G69 class was the final development of the 2-4-2 radial tank on the Great Eastern Railway with larger tanks. Twenty were built at Stratford in 1911-1912 and were readily distinguishable from the earlier types by the inclusion of cab windows. Becoming LNER Class F6, the fleet remained intact well into BR days but withdrawal began in 1955 and the class was extinct within three years. Although No. 67228 was allocated to Lowestoft when photographed at Stratford on 7th July 1956, it was working from Stratford at this time on North Woolwich-Palace Gates trains.

(Below) On 10th March 1956, Stratford-based Class F6 No. 67221 simmers outside Jubilee Shed, having just arrived from duty on the Braintree branch. The Westinghouse pump on the side of the boiler is particularly noticeable in this view as is the ugly stove pipe chimney with which the locomotive has been fitted.

J66 to J69

Prior to the appointment of James Holden as Locomotive Superintendent in 1885, it had been the policy of the Great Eastern Railway to use obsolete main line engines for shunting duties, an unsatisfactory state of affairs in view of the Company's burgeoning freight business. In two and a half years up to the year 1888, 50 of the class, later to become LNER J66, were constructed at Stratford and became the foundation upon which all future GER 0-6-0T designs were based. Pictured at Stratford in April 1954, immediately after withdrawal, No. 68371 was one of the class once used as a shunter at Staveley Works.

The GER Class R24 fleet was built from 1890 and varied from the first 0-6-0Ts by having a wheelbase which was 6in longer, but a rear overhang which was 1ft less, resulting in a shorter engine overall. The side tanks were placed further forward and the cab was slightly smaller. Up to the year 1901, 140 of this type were built with 100 of them being used for suburban passenger duties and the remainder as shunters. One of the fleet classified as J67/1 by the LNER, No. 68516, is seen in use as shed pilot at Stratford on 29th May 1954.

Shown here as a Class J67/2 in 1953, No. 68529 was originally one of the locomotives built in 1892 which received LNER classification J67/1. In 1906 it was rebuilt with the larger 180lb psi boiler and became one of a batch re-classified J69. The engine was given back the smaller 160lb psi boiler in 1938 and, a year after this view, was re-converted yet again to the 180lb type and provided with a fourth classification of J69/1.

The A.J. Hill GER Class C72s became LNER Class J68 and represented the final stage of development of the original Holden 0-6-0Ts. They were fitted with the same 180lb psi boiler as the J69s, but had side window cabs with large square front and rear windows in place of the round ones that were fitted to the other types. No. 68658 was one of the locomotives constructed after the 1923 Grouping and withdrawn in April 1959. It was one of four of the class which were used as shunters at Boston Docks from 1929 until 1953. By 10th March 1956, however, when this photograph was taken, it had returned to Stratford and was carrying the 30A shed plate on the smokebox door.

(Above) At the Grouping, the LNER classified the Holden R24s into categories J67 and J69, denoting the difference in the boilers fitted and the fact that the larger boilered engines also had bigger tanks and fireboxes. One of the larger variety which was originally used for suburban passenger duties, Class J69/1 No. 68527, had the chalked legend 'Ascertain' written at the top of the tank on 11th August 1954, but exactly what was required to be ascertained is not clear.

(Below) Also of Class J69/1, No. 68552, photographed in 1954, still has 'British Railways' just visible on the larger tank sides, has an ugly stove pipe chimney fitted, retains an original wooden cab roof, is absolutely begrimed with dirt – and sports express passenger headcode lamps! Despite its appearance, however, this engine was not destined to be withdrawn from service for another seven years.

(Opposite top) In 1946 one of the Class J67/1 shunting engines with small tanks was fitted with a large firebox boiler pressed to 180lb psi, thus producing yet another variation in the types, and was classified J69/2. Twelve such conversions occurred up to 1953 with No. 68513, shown here on 7th July 1956, having been modified in 1952.

(Opposite bottom) On 5th September 1953, another of the Class J69/2 conversions, No. 68510, is in process of being lifted back onto the tracks following a collision outside New Shed. Damage was minimal however, and the engine remained in service until 1959.

Tram engines designed for use alongside public roads were obliged to comply with Board of Trade regulations and received cow-catchers, protective wheel skirtings, chimney spark arresters, warning bells and a speed governor with an 8mph restriction. J. Holden's GER Class C53 0-6-0Ts were constructed at Stratford betwen 1903 and 1921 and received LNER classification J70. In April 1955 No. 68225 awaits its fate at Stratford having been deposed from Ipswich Docks workings by the then new Drewry diesels.

Of the 81 GER Class S69 4-6-0s constructed, 72 survived to be handed over to BR as Class B12 on Vesting day, and all but four of these received an Eastern Region number in the 60,000 series. Although credited to S.D. Holden, the design was principally the work of the locomotive design section at Stratford headed by F.V. Russell, who succeeded in the task of providing a powerful engine within the strict limitations of length and weight necessary, at the time, to conform with the restrictions of the Great Eastern loading gauge. The situation in this respect was alleviated in many ways by 1931, allowing for an extensive rebuilding of the fleet and providing for a weight increase with a large Gresley pattern boiler. Classified B12/3 on this basis, No. 61519 stands on 30A on 10th March 1956.

The Great Eastern Railway 'Claud Hamilton' 4-4-0s had a particularly chequered career. All 121 of them were constructed at Stratford between 1900 and 1923 and were rebuilt and modified both by the GER and by the LNER over the years, until the locomotives remaining all became classified as D16/3s, but with many variations remaining within them. (Top) on 29th May 1954, No. 62533 has just emerged from Stratford paintshop in unlined black livery and was soon to return to its allocated shed of Melton Constable (32G). This locomotive was a 1933 Gresley rebuild of a D15 with a large round-topped boiler and modified footplating. (Above) No. 62620 was a 1938 rebuild of a D16/2 with the same type of boiler but retaining original slide valves and decorative footplating, and was also a part of the allocation of the ex-Midland & Great Northern Railway shed at Melton Constable when photographed at Stratford on 29th January 1955.

Gresley Types

Although not strictly a Gresley design, the Class K1 Moguls were a Thompson/Peppercorn derivative of the two-cylinder Class K1/1 which, in turn, was a rebuild of a Gresley Class K4 constructed at Darlington in 1938. The 70 locomotives of Class K1 were built by the North British Locomotive Company in the eight months from May 1949 to March 1950 and were considered as versatile machines, handling everything from short trip goods workings to express passenger turns. The last of the class, No. 62005, was withdrawn in December 1967 but was peserved and today is based on the North Yorkshire Moors Railway and works special trains on BR metals to include the Mallaig extension from Fort William. The example here, No. 62032 of March (31B), was not so fortunate and was scrapped following withdrawal in 1963.

The first LNER standard design was the J38 0-6-0 with 4ft 8in wheels, but upon completion of the initial order of 35 locomotives in 1926, no more were built. Instead, further construction of 0-6-0 goods engines was concentrated on a version with 5ft 2in wheels which appeared later the same year and was perpetuated in such numbers, that by 1941 the total stood at 289, making the J39 the most numerous of the many Gresley designs. The class was divided into three parts based upon the type of tender that was attached, with Parts 1 and 2 applying to the LNER 3,500 and 4,200 gallon tenders respectively and Part 3 being reserved for those with miscellaneous tenders from the North Eastern and Great Central Railways. On 19th January 1955, Class J39/3 No. 64977, a Lincoln (40A) engine, has been coaled up at Stratford and awaits the return working home.

Sandringhams

In 1927, Gresley was asked to provide a new class of 4-6-0 passenger engine to supplement the Class B12s on heavier duties. The first ten were constructed by the North British Locomotive Co. with subsequent orders being undertaken by Darlington Works (with some utilisation of Armstrong Whitworth boilers) and Robert Stephensons. By 1936, 73 engines had been built with modifications being introduced with successive batches, in addition to changes in the braking systems and types of tender fitted. (Top) On 22nd August 1954, Class B17/6 No. 61663 *Everton* stands at Stratford adjacent to the Lifting Shed and Mechanical Coaling Plant and is one of the type modified from a B17/4 in 1943 and fitted with a Class B1 type boiler. (Below) London 'Football' rival No. 61648 *Arsenal* has completed duties for the day at Stratford on 25th June 1955 and is a B17/4 fitted with the LNER 4,200 gallon tender. (Above right) Class B17/2 No. 61602 *Walsingham* is one of the type also fitted with a Class B1 boiler and was modified in 1947 from a Class B17/1. (Centre right) No. 61610 *Honingham Hall* is shown on 16th March 1957 and is another Class B17/6 named after English country houses, in this case the home of an LNER Director, Baron Ailwyn, situated between Norwich and Dereham.

(Below) Ten Class B17/1s were rebuilt by Thompson from 1945 as two-cylinder 4-6-0s utilising the Class B1 type boiler and, with one exception, having larger capacity, albeit secondhand, North Eastern Railway tenders taken from withdrawn Class C7 Atlantics and Class P1 Mikados. At Stratford on 7th July 1956, one of the engines rebuilt in this way and classified B2, No. 61603 *Framlingham,* bears a 30E Colchester shed plate but was, in fact, transferred to Cambridge (31A) with the rest of the class in October of that year, all ten remaining on allocation there until their withdrawal in 1958–1959.

The Gresley Class J50 0-6-0Ts were introduced on the Great Northern Railway in 1922 and later adopted by the LNER as good enough for development as one of their standard designs. Thirty smaller-boilered Class J51s were rebuilt to J50s between 1929 and 1935 and all 92 engines passed into BR ownership, withdrawals from traffic beginning in September 1958 and the fleet finally becoming extinct in September 1965 with the cutting-up at Doncaster Works of No. 68961. (Top) One of the post-Grouping engines classified J50/3, No. 68963, is seen at Stratford in June 1953, while (above) No. 68930 was also photographed there in August 1954, its classification J50/2 signifying that this was one of the rebuilt Class J51s. Both locomotives were allocated to 30A for hump shunting the Temple Mills yards.

The first 60 of Gresley's Class N2 0-6-2Ts were constructed for the Great Northern Railway from December 1920 with the remaining 47 appearing as LNER engines after the 1923 Grouping and becoming another of their standard types. Although best remembered for the sterling work they put up on the King's Cross suburban services for almost 40 years, the class were not strangers to Stratford who received their first allocation as long ago as 1929. Between 1952 and 1956, five of the class were allocated to Parkeston (30F) for working the Manningtree-Harwich passenger service and these engines were, naturally, maintained at Stratford where Nos 69566 and 69502 were seen on 23rd April 1955 and 25th June 1955 respectively. The former was classified N2/3, being built without condensing gear, and the latter N2/2, having had the original condensing gear removed.

The ten Great Northern Class H4 Moguls constructed at Darlington in 1920–1921 became LNER Class K3 and were another of Gresley's designs that became a standard type, with a further 183 being built from 1924 to 1937 by Doncaster, Darlington, Armstrong Whitworth, R. Stephenson & Co. and the North British Locomotive Co. It was not until route restrictions were lifted in 1938 that the class were permitted to work on Great Eastern Section metals south of March, when some were transferred to Stratford for working express goods traffic and some passenger turns. No. 61973 (above), was a Lowestoft (32F) engine when photographed at Stratford in January 1955 with No. 61963 (below), being one of the 30A allocation and seen there in May 1954.

Designed by Thompson

The first of Edward Thompson's Class B1 4-6-0s appeared from Darlington Works in December 1942 with the last emerging from the North British Locomotive Co. in April 1952. In all, 410 of the class were constructed for use as Class 5 mixed traffic engines and a number of these were always allocated to Stratford, where they were used on all types of duties from boat trains to humble pick-up goods. On 22nd August 1954, the first of the class, No. 61000 *Springbok*, moves off shed to take out a freight train from Temple Mills to Whitemoor Yard, March.

From when it first emerged from Doncaster Works in 1945, extensive trials were carried out on the first of Thompson's Class L1 2-6-4Ts, prior to further examples being built. It was not until after Nationalisation in 1948 that orders for a further 99 were made, which were constructed over the next two years at BR's Darlington Works, the North British Locomotive Co. and Robert Stephenson & Hawthorns. In the middle 1950s some 20 of the class were allocated to Stratford and they were utilised principally on Hertford East and Bishops Stortford local passenger services. Electrification of the lines from Liverpool Street to Bishops Stortford, Chingford, Enfield and Hertford East in November 1960 resulted in the first 14 of the class being withdrawn, the first being Stratford's No. 67702. The type became extinct when No. 67800 was withdrawn from service in December 1962. On 22nd August 1954, No. 67730 has arrived on Jubilee Shed from working Hertford East trains.

Ex L.T. & S.

Designed by Thomas Whitelegg for the London, Tilbury & Southend Railway and built between 1903 and 1912, all 14 of the 69 class, 3F 0-6-2Ts were subsequently a part of the locomotive stock of the Midland Railway from 1912, the LMS from 1923 and BR from 1948, the first not being withdrawn until 1958 and the last in 1962. On 10th April 1954, No. 41989 simmers outside Jubilee Shed after working in a trip freight from Tilbury Docks to Temple Mills. This locomotive once carried the name *Dagenham Dock*.

Another Whitelegg LT&SR design to survive to BR days was the 79 class, 3P Atlantic Tank, which initially dated from 1897 but was still being built for the LMS as late as 1930. Allocated to Southend Victoria (30D) when photographed at Stratford on the same day, No. 41970 was one of the final batch of ten engines built in 1930, the last of which was finally withdrawn in 1960.

With the large Stratford coaling plant to the rear, one of the 1927 batch of ex-LT&S Class 3P Atlantic Tanks, No. 41944, is seen awaiting entry to the Works on 23rd June 1954 together with a Class N7. Fifty one of the class were built, with the first withdrawal taking place in 1951.

On the same day, ex-LT&S Class 2F 0-6-2T No. 41987 stands in the sunshine in front of an ex-Great Eastern Class J69/1 0-6-0T. In LT&SR days the 0-6-2T was numbered 76 and carried the name *Dunton*. It became Midland Railway No. 2187 circa 1912, LMS No. 2227 after the 1923 Grouping, reverted again to No. 2187 in 1939 and became No. 1987 in 1947 before having 40,000 added to the number by BR.

Atmosphere!

(Opposite top) As it contained no ventilation worthy of the name, it was logical that the six road Stratford New Shed should accommodate the main bulk of repair work for the many engines carrying a 30A shed plate. The much larger Jubilee Shed, with twelve roads was, however, a different sort of place altogether. Although it had a form of ventilation, it also had many more engines in steam, with oil and water endemic. With valve and piston examinations going on, attention being given to Westinghouse brake pumps and other minor repairs undertaken, it had a reputation for fumes and vapour that could, at times, be exceedingly unpleasant. On the warm evening of 22nd August 1954, there is little breeze to blow away the 'atmosphere' as four locomotives simmer in the sun. From left to right are Class K3/2 Mogul No. 61830, Class B2 4-6-0 No. 61616 *Fallodon,* another Class K3/2, No. 61862 and Class N7/1 0-6-2T No. 69624.

(Opposite bottom) There was continuous activity around the Stratford coaling plant and coal dust was, naturally, everywhere. In choking atmosphere, Class Y4 0-4-0T No. 68127 is flanked by two Class F5 2-4-2Ts on 8th May 1953.

(Above) The sulphureous fumes emitting from Jubilee Shed on 10th March 1956 almost obliterate the Class B1 tender to the rear of this view of two Stratford Class F5 2-4-2Ts Nos 67209 and 67211.

(Below) A typical smokey scene outside Jubilee Shed with some locomotives arriving from their labours and others about to depart. In this view on 10th April 1954 can be seen the front end of a Class B1, the rear of a 'Britannia', Class K3/2 No. 61973, Class L1 No. 67713 and Class J68 No. 68652. The northern half of Jubilee Shed, containing roads 7 to 12, was eventually demolished to make way for a depot to accommodate new diesel locomotives.

With passenger services arriving at Liverpool Street station and freight coming into Temple Mills, many locomotives allocated to sheds other than Stratford utilised the depot services and, during the latter part of the 1950s, it was not unknown for some 'foreigners' in good order to be sequestrated for long periods. On 5th September 1953, Class J19 0-6-0 No. 64667 and Class J39/3 No. 64789 await replenishment of coal and water before returning to their home bases of Colchester (30E) and Peterborough Spital Bridge (35C) respectively.

Fitted with a window cab for working the Colne Valley line and also having a back cab, Class J15 0-6-0 No. 65424 is coaled up ready to return home to Colchester while, to the rear, 'Sandringham' No. 61608 *Gunton* has its smokebox cleared.

(Opposite bottom) A visitor from the large Peterborough shed of New England (35A) on 11th August 1954 was Ivatt LMS Class 4MT Mogul No. 43058. The letters 'SC' below the shed plate denoted that the locomotive was fitted with a self-cleaning smokebox.

Hauling a transfer freight from Temple Mills Yard, Class B1 4-6-0 No. 61006 *Blackbuck* of Parkeston shed (30F), takes the line west of the Stratford shed complex on 10th April 1954 and approaches Victoria Park Junction. The 'New Works' building can be seen in the left background.

In the mid-1950s the fleet of Class J19 0-6-0s was allocated exclusively to Stratford and Cambridge Divisions and they all worked in and out of Stratford at different times. Allocated to Colchester shed (30E), No. 64645 awaits a return freight from Temple Mills on 28th June 1952.

On a very dull and misty morning in October 1955, Class WD 2-8-0 No. 90454 from New England (35A) cautiously steams through High Meads Junction, Stratford, and heads a freight towards the North London Line.

In 1950, Stratford Works commenced the overhaul of Ivatt ex-Great Northern Class N1 0-6-2Ts instead of Doncaster, and even locomotives allocated to sheds in the West Riding of Yorkshire came down for the purpose. On the murky day of 23rd January 1954, No. 69447 from Bradford (37C), has received an accidental scrape to its freshly applied paintwork and waits to return to Works for this to be touched out before returning northwards.

Class J69/1 0-6-0T No. 68629 comes off the Channelsea curve into Stratford High Level station shortly after daybreak on 5th September 1953, hauling two 'Royal Mail' coaches that have found themselves in the area.

Still awaiting fitting of a new round-topped boiler and still, in consequence, classified J20 instead of J20/1, 0-6-0 No. 64698 is seen at Stratford on 22nd August 1954 whilst a part of the March (31B) allocation.

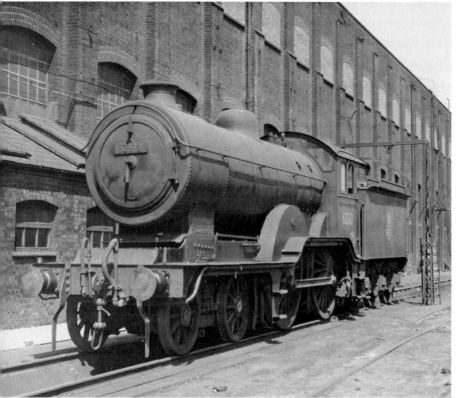

Allocated to Bury St. Edmunds shed (31E), Class D16/3 4-4-0 No. 62513 awaits attention outside the Works on 8th August 1953. At least four of this class were usually allocated to Bury St. Edmunds, right up to the time when they were displaced by the new diesel multiple units in 1957.

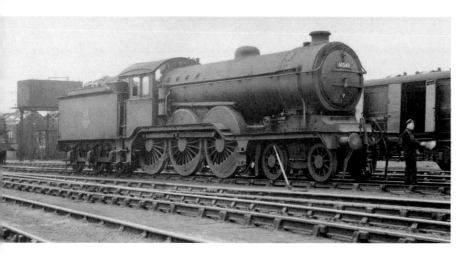

After additional motive power became available on the Great Eastern Section of the Eastern Region, in the shape of new Class B1 and ex-Great Central allocated B17 4-6-0s, a gradual concentration of Class B12/3s took place at Stratford, where the engines monopolised the Liverpool Street-Southend Victoria trains during the 1950s. Allocated to Southend Victoria shed (30D), when this view of No. 61549 was taken at Stratford on 29th May 1954, the engine was ready to take out such a working.

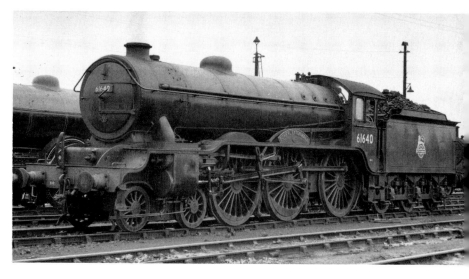

Although having been allocated to sheds such as Lincoln, Colwick, Gorton and Leicester, all the remaining 'Sandringham' 4-6-0s had returned to the Great Eastern Section of the Eastern Region by 1951, where they saw out their days to 1960, when the last to be withdrawn was No. 61668 *Bradford City*. On 11th August 1954, No. 61640 *Somerleyton Hall* was photographed at Stratford whilst allocated to Cambridge (31A). Somerleyton Hall is situated near Lowestoft and is the residence of Baron Somerleyton.

In the same way as the class B17s, a number of the Class J17 0-6-0s roamed from their original Great Eastern environment and, during the Second World War, were a part of the allocation of such diverse sheds as New England, Boston, Grantham, Hornsey and King's Cross. All returned to Great Eastern metals however, during 1943 and, apart from the occasional sojourn to Midland & Great Northern and London, Tilbury & Southend lines, they saw their days out attached to Stratford, Cambridge and Norwich Districts, until becoming one of the many victims of the East Anglian dieselisation programme. On 23rd April 1955, No. 65582 of King's Lynn (31C) has just been hauled from Stratford Works after a major overhaul and repaint and was, in fact, one of the last three of the class to be withdrawn in September 1962. No. 65567, however, has been preserved as LNER No. 1217E.

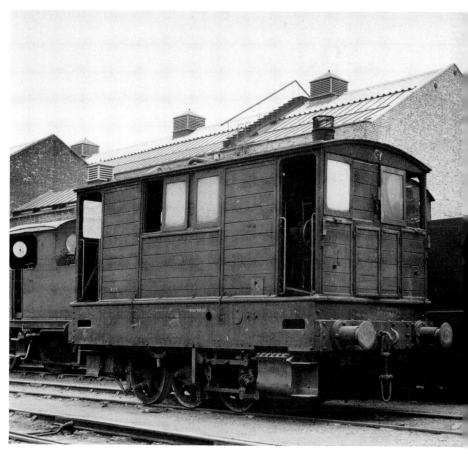

After withdrawal of passenger services on the Wisbech & Upwell line on the last day of 1927, two Class J70 0-6-0Ts were sufficient to cope with the remaining freight traffic but Wisbech, a sub-shed to March (31B), actually maintained an allocation of five of the small fleet until 1948. Drewry diesel mechanical shunters made their debut on the Tramway in 1952 and the last steam working was supposed to have run on 4th July of that year. However No. 68222 was retained for emergency purposes and was subsequently needed on a number of occasions before finally leaving in March 1953. Taken out of service in January 1955, the locomotive awaits cutting-up outside Stratford Works on 23rd April of that year, having been withdrawn from Ipswich, its final base.

Profiles

(Top) In many instances, photography of engines on shed was restricted by cramped conditions that frequently prevailed and a locomotive profile was not always possible. Despite the many engines always to be seen at Stratford, however, the space available there was usually sufficient for a 'portrait' of this nature. This example of Class F5 2-4-2T No. 67192 was taken in January 1955.

(Above) The handsome lines of Class K1 Mogul No. 62037 are displayed to advantage in this profile of the engine taken at Stratford on 13th September 1957.

Paired with an LNER Standard 3,500 gallon tender, Class J39/1 0-6-0 No. 64772 displays its rather chunky appearance to the camera on 29th May 1954.

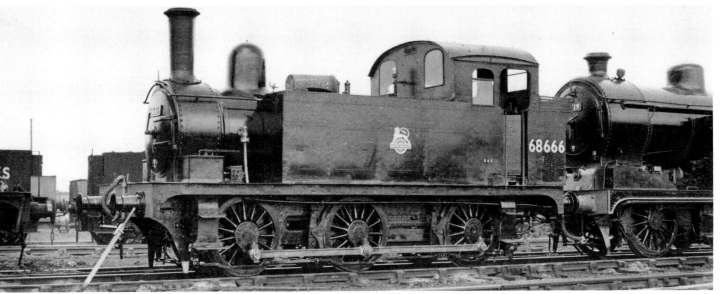

(Top) With the wheels spaced quite wide apart, the design of the Class J20 0-6-0s resulted in a somewhat stretched appearance when viewed in profile. No. 64676 was recorded at Stratford in January 1955.

(Above) The very last of the numerous Great Eastern 0-6-0Ts to be constructed was Class J68 No. 68666 which emerged from Stratford Works in November 1923 as GER No. 7040. Following overhaul and repaint at Stratford in April 1955, the spruce little engine will soon be coaled and watered and returned to traffic.

A sleek profile is provided by Class 3P Atlantic Tank No. 41952 at Stratford on 10th April 1954.

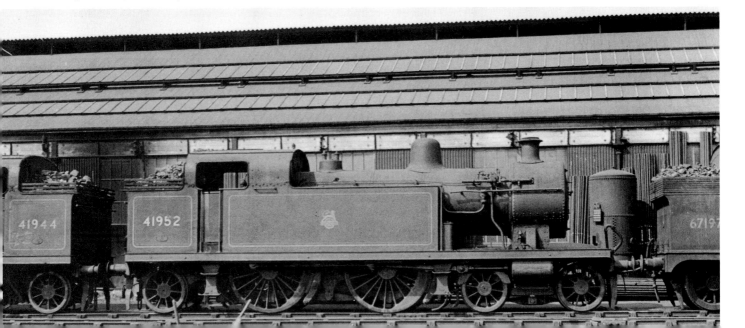

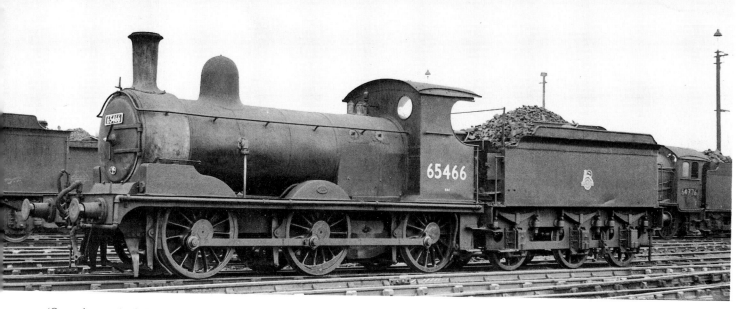

(Opposite top) Originally intended for use on suburban passenger duties, Class J69/1 0-6-0T No. 68549 was fitted with 1,200 gallon tanks and the cab and bunker widened to suit when rebuilt from an R24 Class (J67/1) in 1906. The mess of equipment attached to the boiler in front of the tank indicates that this locomotive is dual fitted with a vacuum ejector added to the Westinghouse system.

(Opposite middle) Possibly a precursor to the present day Stratford liking for individualistic embellishments to their charges, is the painting of the smokebox hinges on 'Sandringham' Class B17/6 No. 61645 *The Suffolk Regiment*, seen at the 'front' end of Jubilee Shed waiting to take its leave in January 1955.

(Opposite bottom) Despite the high running plate and mass of exposed piping, the R.A. Riddles BR Standard 'Britannia' Pacifics still presented themselves as a good looking, well-balanced engine as witness No. 70041 *Sir John Moore* at Stratford in September 1955. Observe the contrast with normal height running plates on the Class WD 2-8-0 to the rear.

The meduim-length cast iron chimney was, arguably, the most suited of the various types that were fitted to the T.W.Worsdell Class J15 0-6-0s over the years. In handsome profile, No. 65466 hardly looks its 56 years of age in August 1955.

By providing S.D. Holden's Great Eastern design of 4-6-0 with a large, round-topped boiler and long-travel valves, and removing the decorative valancing, Gresley did nothing to enhance the original appearance of the locomotives but certainly performance was improved. On the 7th July 1956, the casing of B12/3 No. 61579 is quite hot to the touch under a mid-day summer sun.

Although it was early March, Class J15 0-6-0 No. 65370 still carried a Cowlairs-type snowplough fitted to the front bufferbeam, with the buffers removed, when photographed at Stratford in 1956. Broadly speaking this class could be divided into two categories, those built up to the end of 1890 with level grates, and the ones constructed from 1891 with sloping grates. This division of the types was important for maintenance purposes as the two designs of boiler were not interchangeable. However, this particular locomotive, although one of the pre-1891 engines, had modified frames in order to take a boiler with a sloping grate.

When seen outside Jubilee Shed on 11th August 1954, Class J17 0-6-0 No. 65552 had only a few months life remaining, as withdrawal took place in the following January. This locomotive was one of just 17 of the class that were fitted with vacuum ejectors and steam heat connections, between 1942 and 1951 for working passenger trains on the Midland & Great Northern Section where they replaced withdrawn Joint Line engines. Constructed with the intention of working only loose-coupled goods trains, the class otherwise, were fitted with just steam brakes.

With the exception of Departmental No. 33. the small fleet of Class Y4 0-4-0Ts was replaced by 0-4-0 diesel locomotives in the middle 1950s, and withdrawal of No. 68125 took place in September 1955. This photograph of the engine was taken just under one year earlier in October 1954.

Stratford's only Class 9F 2-10-0 No. 92014 is seen against a background of the Stratford 'coaler' on 11th August 1954. Five different types of tender were attached to this class, depending to a large extent upon the region to which the locomotives were allocated, this particular tender being classified BRIF.

30A Steam at Work

At Liverpool Street

On 7th October 1951, Class B12/3 4-6-0 No. 61575 makes a rousing exit from Liverpool Street station with a Sunday service for Southend Victoria.

Class L1 2-6-4T No. 67729 approaches the ex-Great Eastern Railway's London terminus of Liverpool Street on 25th April 1951. As a result of their distinctive clanking motion, these locomotives were given the nickname of 'Cement Mixers'.

1st July 1952 was a hot, hazy day at Liverpool Street. On the left, Class B17/1 4-6-0 'Sandringham' No. 61608 *Gunton* of 30A awaits departure time with the 12.50pm train for Southend while, in the opposite platform, Class B12/3 4-6-0 No. 61535 from 32B waits to return home to Ipswich with a parcels train.

It has long been a tradition for the Liverpool Street station pilot to receive a livery distinctive from all others allocated to 30A, and today a 1960 built Class 08 shunter painted in Great Eastern Railway livery holds sway. In the early 1950s, this Class J69/1 0-6-0T was returned to its LNER numbering of E8619 and painted in LNER green but with Nationalisation having taken place only a few years before, no one was yet brave enough to include the letters LNER on the tank sides, a compromise being made by using the original BR style of lettering undertaken prior to design of the first 'lion and wheel' emblem.

Prior to the advent of the BR Standard Pacific locomotives, the principal Norwich/Yarmouth expresses were often handled by one of Stratford's Class B1 4-6-0s. On 25th April 1951, No. 61130 arrives at its destination hauling Gresley stock.

Even in the 1950s some train passengers still stuck their heads from carriage windows and stared at the camera! On 11th April 1951, Class B1 No. 61205 makes a lively start from Liverpool Street station with an express for Cromer.

The rays of a low winter sun filter through the Liverpool Street station roof on 25th February 1953, as Class N7/5 0-6-2T No. 69687 impatiently blows off steam while awaiting departure time with the 12.26pm local train for Hertford East.

Having arrived earlier in the day with a semi-fast service from Ipswich, one of the 'Sandringham' 4-6-0s named after well known football clubs, Class B17/4 No. 61661 *Sheffield Wednesday*, uses the Liverpool Street station turntable on 11th May 1951 in order to handle a return working.

Class J68 0-6-0T No. 68644 rattles across the points outside Liverpool Street station on 25th April 1951, returning to Thornton Fields carriage sidings, Stratford, after bringing in a rake of empty coaching stock.

Goods Traffic of the 1950s

Passing a Class 306 electric multiple unit on a Liverpool Street-Shenfield service which is nearing its destination, Class B1 No. 61249 *FitzHerbert Wright* races down the bank towards Brentwood at Ingrave on 30th June 1954 with a motley collection of parcels vans

Veteran Class J15 0-6-0 No. 65370 slowly moves a mixed freight away from Temple Mills Yard on 10th April 1954 bound for Colchester. This locomotive was withdrawn from service two years after this view was taken, but one of the class is today preserved and operates trains on the North Norfolk Railway as LNER No. 7564 (BR No. 65462).

Between Shenfield and Brentwood on 30th June 1954, a very short 'pick-up' vans train is hustled towards London by Class B12/3 4-6-0 No. 61549.

A work-stained Class B1 4-6-0 No. 61052 climbs Brentwood Bank on 9th May 1953 with vans for Harwich Parkeston Quay.

Although giving the appearance of a single track branch line, this location is actually the Southend main line loop between Brentwood and Mountnessing Junction. On 10th May 1952, Class J20/1 No. 64677 drifts through with an eastbound loose-coupled freight.

A southbound engineers' train passes Bishops Stortford on 27th April 1952 powered by Class L1 2-6-4T No. 67723. The train consists of two staff accommodation coaches, five ballast wagons and a brakevan and, at first, gave the appearance of being a rare mixed working.

With freight for Goodmayes Yard, Belpaire-boilered Class J20 No. 64686 saunters down the bank towards Brentwood station on 5th September 1953.

Local Services

On 8th August 1953 the Palace Gates – North Woolwich train departs from Stratford (Low Level) behind bunker-first Class F5 2-4-2T No. 67219.

The train for North Woolwich waits to leave Palace Gates station on 10th April 1954 behind another of the 30A Class F5 2-4-2Ts, No. 67209. Palace Gates station, together with Noel Park and West Green, was closed in January 1963.

The Stratford Class F5s, which were fitted for push-pull working, were used principally on the Epping-Ongar auto trains. Having just watered up at Epping station, No. 67213 is ready to return to Ongar with the 11.32am service.

Stratford's two road sub-shed at Epping is more remembered for the Class F4 and F5 Ongar push-pull tanks than for Class J15s or even a C12, but these types were the only locomotives to be seen there when this view was taken on 8th August 1953. The Class J15 0-6-0s were utilised for freight workings to Ongar from either Temple Mills or Epping while the ex-Great Northern Railway Class C12 4-4-2T was one of a small number fitted for push-pull operation which was tried on the branch, but with little success. The shed closed and the steam services ceased on 18th November 1957 when the London Transport Underground system was extended through to Ongar.

Class N7/5 0-6-2T No. 69662 restarts its train of Gresley 'Quinart' stock, which forms the 3.38pm Enfield Town-Liverpool Street, from Stamford Hill station on 4th June 1958.

With the raised parts of the smokebox door picked out in silver and the number background in red, further indication of Stratford's individualistic ways are apparent on Class N7/5 0-6-2T No. 69669. It pauses at Bethnal Green station on the same day as the above with the 6.27pm Liverpool Street-Enfield Town train which is also made up of 'Quinart' stock.

Hauling a local service for Liverpool Street, begrimed Class L1 2-6-4T No. 67726 heads south from Bishops Stortford on 27th April 1952, the young lady at lineside appearing quite oblivious to the proceedings.

The 10.16am Epping-Ongar service is propelled through the Essex countryside near North Weald on 8th August 1953 by Class F5 2-4-2T No. 67200.

On the Main Line

BR Standard 'Britannia' Pacific No. 70003 *John Bunyan* steams easily up the 1 in 85 section of Brentwood Bank on 9th May 1953 hauling the heavy 'Norfolkman' express from Liverpool Street to Norwich.

With the coaches of the train belying the locomotive's express headcode, Class B1 4-6-0 No. 61006 *Blackbuck* races down Brentwood Bank on the same day heading for Liverpool Street.

Approaching Mountnessing Junction and passing under the Norwich main line between Shenfield and Billericay on 10th May 1952, Class B12/3 4-6-0 No. 61546 carries the distinctive discs which denote that this is an express service from Liverpool Street to Southend Victoria.

Raising the dust on the decent from Ingrave Summit, BR Standard Pacific No. 70000 *Britannia* runs early with the London bound "Hook Continental" from Harwich Parkeston Quay on 9th May 1953.

(Opposite top) Carrying Southend express discs, Class B17/4 'Footballer' No. 61648 *Arsenal* climbs to Ingrave Summit with the 8.45am service for Southend Victoria in May 1953. Class B17s bearing the names of the three big London football clubs represented by No. 61630 *Tottenham Hotspur* and No. 61672 *West Ham*, in addition to *Arsenal*, were all allocated to 30A at this time and all three appeared to have an edge in cleanliness over the remainder of the class which were allocated there. It is likely that football rivalry among the engine cleaners had something to do with it!

(Opposite bottom) Climbing towards Ingrave Summit from Shenfield on the evening of 30th June 1954, 'Britannia' Pacific No. 70036 *Boadicea* has charge of a Liverpool Street express from Sheringham and Cromer, two East Anglian coastal resorts which are today served only by a local stopping train from Norwich. Despite electrification and dieselisation, it was much more convenient to travel to Cromer or Sheringham in the 1950s than it is today and taking into account a good express running time to Cromer was then 3 hr 20 min, the journey is not very much faster today either!

On the main line near Harold Wood in June 1954, a Class J20/1 0-6-0 No. 64677 with round-topped boiler, has an easy task hauling just two vans and a brake. The load will become heavier as the journey to Ipswich progresses, however, as the train is scheduled to pick up other wagons from stations along the way.

Unusual motive power for a Liverpool Street-Southend express on 8th August 1953 was Class K3/2 Mogul No. 61840, pictured here at speed through Forest Gate in East London.

Rounding the curve between Stansted and Bishops Stortford on 27th April 1952, Class B17/1 4-6-0 No. 61600 *Sandringham* heads for Liverpool Street with an express from Cambridge.

The initial electrification from Liverpool Street in early 1950 finished just north of Shenfield, where this photograph was taken on 10th May 1952, of 'Britannia' Pacific No. 70003 *John Bunyan* hauling an express from Liverpool Street to Norwich and Yarmouth.

The 5.52pm train from King's Cross to Cambridge and Abbots Ripton was always double headed in the 1950s, with one locomotive taking the Abbots Ripton portion on after detaching at Hitchin. The other half of the train was then taken on to Cambridge by the other locomotive. It was not often that a 30A engine was used on the service but on 7th April 1954 the two B1 Class 4-6-0s hammering up Holloway Bank from King's Cross were No. 61113 from Doncaster (35A) and No. 61233 from Stratford.

With apologies to any reader who has seen this photograph in print before, but it is one of my personal favourites and ideally suitable for the final page of this album. On 11th March 1952, 'Britannia' Pacific No. 70002 *Geoffrey Chaucer* prepares to leave Liverpool Street with the "East Anglian" express for Norwich. Leaving London at 6.30pm, the train was timed to arrive at Norwich Thorpe at 8.40pm, a running time of 2 hr 10 min.